INTRODUCTION

In choosing Walkley for my next book in the *Camera* series I became aware of two facts. [...] rather there was a dichotomy to the area. In the lower part that slopes down to Langsett Road the houses were of a poor standard. Not to put too fine a point on it they were slums and as such have been demolished these thirty years or more. Higher up - say from Walkley Road and above - the dwellings were more spacious and built to a better standard and these have mostly survived which takes me to my second fact that some photographs taken many years ago are not very different from a photograph taken today. Now no-one wants to pay hard-earned cash for a book of photos that they could easily take themselves.

So I have concentrated in the main on scenes that have changed. This has not been too difficult so far as black-and-white photographs are concerned but for colour - well to be frank much of old Walkley does not immediately encourage the use of colour film and so for the colour section I have used photographs that emphasised the more picturesque parts of the area and there are plenty of those.

I have also, for the first time, included a map. The reason is that much of Lower Walkley has now disappeared without trace. When Attercliffe was re-developed in the 1960s and 1970s much of the old road layout remained after the houses had gone but that did not happen to Walkley. The bulldozers moved in and swept away the lot. It is not possible now to go and point out where Grammar Street, Freedom Street, Burnaby Street, Hattersley Street, Gould Street, Majuba Street and others used to be. The map is taken from an old street directory and may help you to find your way about.

On a couple of occasions I have mentioned the name of Tommy Fogg. Tommy contacted me after buying a copy of my "A Hillsborough Camera". He spent his boyhood in Greaves Street and when he learned that my next book was to be about Walkley he enthusiastically went through my "possibles" and was able to identify some locations and generously share some of his memories with me.

A few of these photographs might well have made it into my Hillsborough book. Langsett Road could well be said to qualify for either. However, I have not duplicated any of them. Fortunately I have a wealth of images to choose from of Langsett Road and its tributary streets - some dating back over a hundred years. I hope some day to be able to put them together in another book.

Acknowledgements:
With thanks to David Richardson for the use of photographs from his collection and through him C.J. Farrant.

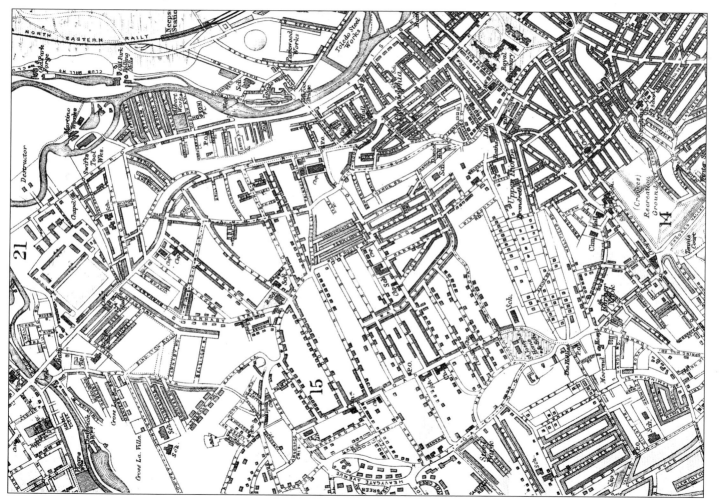

This is Hammerton Road Police Station - one of the few old stations left in Sheffield. It probably dates from around 1930 but its hour of fame came when the Yorkshire Ripper, Peter Sutcliffe, was finally caught in Sheffield after a series of murders of women. He probably still regrets the night he wandered from his home area of Bradford into Sheffield where he was apprehended by the Late Sergeant Robert Ring and P.C. Robert Hydes while doing a routine patrol near Glossop Road on Friday January 2nd 1981. The young lady he was with had a lucky escape and he was brought to Hammerton Road before it was realised who they had in custody. He was found to be criminally insane and is now "detained during Her Majesty's Pleasure".

Burnaby Street runs downhill from Walkley Road to Langsett Road. This is how it looked back in the 1970s with terraced houses aplenty and children with the handy Walkley School (right) on the doorstep. Pretty well all on this picture is now grass.

5

Walkley School straddles Burnaby Street and Greaves Street. When this photograph was taken in July 1974 on a wet afternoon it was still a school serving the closely knit community of lower Walkley. Since most of that went it has now become a hostel for University students.

This is the view that generations of Walkley kids would have seen in gazing through the school railings of Walkley School at any time between the 1870s and the 1960s. They would have been looking towards the junction of Walkley Road and Freedom Road with, on the left, the Freedom pub. This photo dates from the 1970s.

This is Greaves St. with Walkley County School on the right. The date is July 1974. In the distance is Langsett Road. The area below the school has all been cleared of masses of houses. On a recent visit I found the school still in use but considerably extended.

The shop selling Lyons' Cakes stood at the corner of Walkley Road and Burnaby Street when this was taken in April 1974. In its place there is now a copse of trees.

Here is Walkley Road at the top of Burnaby Street showing two lost pubs. On the right is the Royal Oak and left is The Freedom. On a recent visit The Freedom had been demolished and a new building was under construction. The Royal Oak is now a private house. This photo dates from 1974.

This photograph was taken from Woodview Rd. and looks down towards Hillsborough Barracks. It is only from here that one gets an idea of the huge acreage it occupied.

Here you are looking down Woodland Street towards Langsett Road.

Tommy Fogg remembers that the white building with the nearer van parked outside sold ice cream. The date of the photograph is 13th September 1965.

In researching this book I have been surprised how many people remember the Spiritualist church that was approached up this passage on Woodland Street.
The little notice guided the way in, 1970.

Channing Street is here viewed from Langsett Road back in 1970. The street ran uphill eventually meeting Burnaby Street just below the school. All this has now disappeared completely being replaced by new houses called Channing Gardens. On the right was Patnick's shop opposite the Post Office.

Here we are looking down Channing Street in 1970. Prominent in the centre is the massive Wycliffe chapel that was in two parts. The other came out onto Langsett Rd. It is a reminder of how attached to non-conformist chapels people were in Victorian times.

Looking down Channing Street once again, but this time a little higher up on 13th September 1965. These little courtyards were a common feature in Victorian times.

Grammar St. in 1970. The road to the right is Normandale Rd. that runs downhill to join Langsett Road. The shops in the distance are at the corner of Greaves St. See page 31 for a closer view of the shop.

This was Freedom Street - now lost without trace. The houses number from 28 upwards. In the distance Channing Street can be seen. My 1963 Kelly's directory tells me the following:

28 Jack Tranter
30 Mrs B. Machin
32 John Tranter
34 Mrs A. Stringer
36 J. Hyde
38 Eric Crownshaw

at which point the directory lets me down - so who owned the little shop at the corner of Channing St. and what did they sell?

These courtyards were a feature of lower Grammar St. near Langsett Road. The house on the right is No. 153 and you are looking down No. 13 court. My Kelly's does not give the name of the occupant.

The White Horse pub was at 19 Grammar Street. Across the road at No. 22 Grammar St. stood the Victoria Inn pub (see page 23) There was a good deal of friendly rivalry between the two hostelries and an annual football match took place between them on the waste ground that can be seen at the side of the pub. This is another 1970 photo.

I was standing on Grammar Street on 13th September 1965 when I took this photograph of the backyards here seen with the weekly wash drying on the line. The backyards are probably on King James St. but I would welcome confirmation of this.

This pub on South Road was known by locals as the "Top Freedom" to distinguish it from the "Bottom Freedom" shown on pages 10 and 42. The two "Freedoms" owe their name to a building society "The Freedom Hill Land Society". see Peter Harvey's Book on street names.

The Victoria Inn, No. 22 Grammar Street as it was around 1965. All has now gone but I hope the two young ladies recognise themselves - they could even be grandmothers!

This was Greaves Street in 1970 shortly before the street was cleared. on the right below the police box is Langsett Road. The road running off to the left is Bradley Place. Some of the houses are already boarded up awaiting their fate.

This is Freedom Street and in the distance is Burnaby Street. On the right are back-to-back houses. Notice the street wall-lamp. The date is 13th September 1965.

This was Greaves St. after demolition had begun. The lower part had been cleared but had revealed back-to back houses with an extra yard behind into which even more houses had been crammed. Tommy Fogg lived in one of the back-to-back houses and he has been very helpful in adding life to some of these old Victorian streets. He recalls that the little shop - just visible - could be relied upon for a small loan if you were desperate. 1970 again.

Everything in this picture has now gone. I was standing in Grammar Street. The road downhill is a continuation of Grammar St. down to Langsett Rd. The street that carries the nameplate is Freedom St. Running in front of the wall to the left is Greaves St. The date of the photograph is 1970.

Bradley Place between Grammar Street and Greaves St. in 1967. Already two of the houses have their windows boarded up. Many of these boarded up windows carried the message "EL OFF" which I at first took to be a warning to intruders but later learned that it only signified that the electric supply had been disconnected.

This photograph from 1970 shows where Grammar St. joined
Langsett Rd. The building in use by Hawley's Tyres was formerly a
public house - The Royal Exchange.
In the 1915 Directory the landlord was a Mr. Joseph Exley.
Sam Eales' Crown Garage can be seen on the extreme left.

Grammar Street taken from Langsett Road in 1970. The posters make interesting reading. George Darling was M.P. for the Hillsborough Ward at the time. His most illustrious predecessor was A.V. Alexander who became First Lord of the Admiralty under Winston Churchill throughout most of the Second World War. Other well-known Hillsborough MPs are Martin Flannery, a local schoolmaster, and Helen Jackson - the sitting M.P. This photo gives a better view of the Crown Garage.

You will not know Hattersley Street any more than I did unless you lived there for it is not to be found either on my old Geographia A1 Atlas or in my Kelly's Directories. Tommy Fogg put me wise. The street ran from Grammar Street with two even smaller streets running off to the right. The nearer one was Gould Street and the more distant one was Poplar Street. I see that the shop is selling Craven A cigarettes - once a popular brand now only remembered by us oldies. The shop on the left was at the corner of Grammar Street.

This picture of Majuba Street was taken in 1965.

I have spoken to many Walkley folk but none of them remember this street.

It was to be found immediately below what is now the Infants School.

It took its name from Majuba Hill in South Africa where an action against the Boers took place in 1881. (See Peter Harvey's book "Street Names of Sheffield".)

I believe this to be Creswick Street where it joined Langsett Road. Foolishly I only labelled the photograph as "Langsett Road" and it is now difficult to differentiate the innumerable roads that swept down from lower Walkley into Langsett Road before the whole of lower Walkley was cleared for the new Langsett estate.

This is a view of Primrose Hill from Whitehouse Lane looking down towards Langsett Road. The piece of waste land was a popular playground for local kids and was known as the Rec. St. Bartholomew's church schoolroom is to be seen. This is another pic from my 1970 outing.

Burgoyne Road. St. Bartholomew's Sunday School outing. c1912

This photograph of Burgoyne Road dates from 11th September 1965. The large church was St. Bartholomew's and extended right across to Primrose Hill where its Sunday School was to be found. The whole complex was demolished and a new smaller church has been built along with number of small flats.

This telephoto view was taken from Parkwood Springs on the 8th August 1983. The school that dominates the picture is Burgoyne Road Board School. The road on the left is Burgoyne Road and on the right is Cundy Street. Sheffield created many such massive schools in the 1870s to cater for the introduction of compulsory education. Unfortunately some of them have gone and others are under threat.

This is the best photograph I have showing St. Bartholomew's church in total. We are here looking down Primrose Hill with the Sunday School on the left and the church to the right with its entrance on Burgoyne Road. The date is around 1975 since when it has all been demolished.

Many of the buildings along Whitehouse Lane shown here as they were on 24th July 1974 have now disappeared. Everything in the left foreground as far as Burgoyne Road has gone. Likewise the imposing detached house at the upper right hand corner of Burgoyne Road has also gone. Whitehouse Lane takes its name from the White House that stood somewhere above Burgoyne Road.

Whitehouse Lane crosses Burgoyne Road running off to the right of the photograph. The buildings below Burgoyne Road have all gone and the beer-off shop is now a private house. The photo dates from the early 1970s.

Another more recent view of Burgoyne Road school taken from below to emphasise its domination of the area. Its stone face has been cleaned about which their are conflicting views but if such attention means that it is to be preserved I shall be glad.

Although taken only a few years ago this pub on Walkley Road has now
disappeared. When I visited the site a completely new building was being built.
For a photograph of it in action as it were (see page 10) where barrels of beer
for thirsty customers were being
unloaded back in 1970.

A recent photograph of Martin Street with its imposing high rise tower blocks going in steps down towards the site of the old Royal Infirmary. They have done well to last for nearly forty years. To see how Martin Street used to be see page 60

Moor End House as it now stands - but for how much longer. There was at one time an extension as can be seen from the lighter colour of the stonework. Since it was a family home it has been in use for various purposes but I fear it may now be doomed - let us hope not. See page 72 to see it in its heyday.

The Hallamshire House is a pretty old pub on Commonside standing opposite The Closed Shop pub. Notice the little period cottage attached.

The name of this pub smacks of politics but Michael Liversidge's book, A to Z of Sheffield Public Houses, tells me that it was inspired because at one time the licence was withheld and the public house had to close for a time. It stands on Commonside.

A view of lower Walkley taken from Parkwood Springs in 1980. Very little of old Walkley has survived. The Infants School that was on Greaves St. has been spruced up but the area above Langsett Rd, has gone forever.

Rivelin St. was part of the old Racker Way that led down to Rivelin and then up and over the Pennines to Manchester. It is terribly steep for most of the way and one's heart bleeds for the poor pack animals that had to make the journey in all weathers. On a sunny autumn day like this it is a beautiful view.

When I took this photograph around 1975 it was more as an artistic roofscape than as a record but now I am sure it is Hawksworth Road.

This corner beer-off shop stood at the corner of Addy St. and Albion St.
The fact that one window has been bricked up due to the window tax dates the
shop well back into Victorian times. The photograph was taken on 25th August
1965.

No. 27 Blakegrove Rd. was the home of Ebenezer Elliott - see the plaque below. When he had this house built it was well out in the country, but of course, no longer.

CITY OF SHEFFIELD
EBENEZER ELLIOTT
THE CORN LAW RHYMER
1781-1849
LIVED HERE
1834-1841

This was how Addy St. looked back in 1965. The wreck of a car gives it quite a modern look but all these houses have now gone. The pub was at the corner of Cross Addy St. and was the Victoria Hotel (Number 80-82). Cross St. led into Springvale Rd.

THE KELVIN DEVELOPMENT c1961

I have joined together two photographs to give some idea of the area that was cleared to make room for the Kelvin Flats development. The join is not perfect but the photograph is probably unique. I have indicated the street names in ink. They are - from left to right - Kelvin St., Woollen Lane, Robert St. and Edith St. Beyond these is Infirmary Road. I was probably standing on Jenkinson Street when I took the photographs.

Where the previous photograph left off this scene continues looking at the Kelvin development. We are at the junction of Langsett Road and Infirmary Road with Whitehouse Lane running across. It was taken at the same time as the previous photograph.

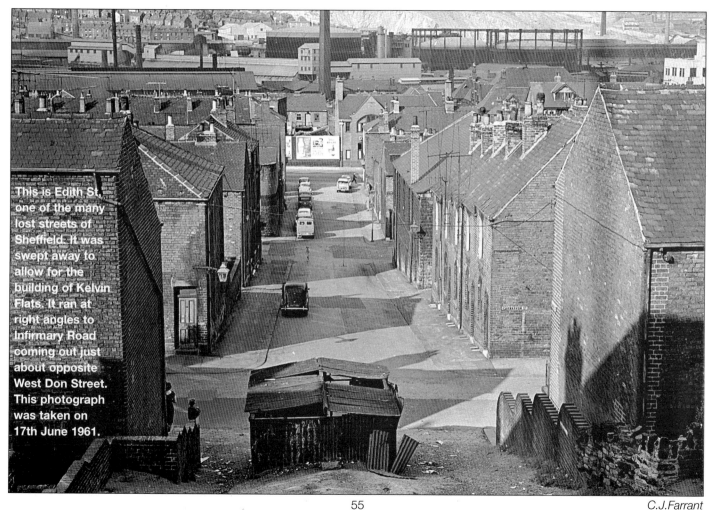

This is Edith St. one of the many lost streets of Sheffield. It was swept away to allow for the building of Kelvin Flats. It ran at right angles to Infirmary Road coming out just about opposite West Don Street. This photograph was taken on 17th June 1961.

C.J.Farrant

The Huge Kelvin Flats development seemed forever immovable but after forty years of life they went.

One benefit to photographers was that they provided a useful viewpoint for overlooking the area.

This photograph was in fact taken from the flats where they made a right angle turn and show what was left of Carnarvon Street.

The date was 1978.

Oxford Street as it was on 25th August 1965. Filling the background is what was once the old Oxford Picture Palace. The building was originally a Unitarian chapel but became a cinema in 1913. When this photograph was taken it was in use as a car sales lot - hence the many motor cars.

This gives a wider view of the area from Upperthorpe towards the Kelvin Flats. The Scarborough Arms and the library are survivors of an area that has undergone much development since this photograph was taken in May 1974.

This view of Upperthorpe shows a little known business that has now disappeared. Just above the library industrial premises can be seen and these belonged to the only firm of coopers or barrel makers that existed in Sheffield. They made wooden barrels for the brewing trade before the newer metal barrels came into use. Its name was The Sheffield Cooperage Ltd.
The date of this photo was May 1974.

This was Martin Street in 1902 decked out to celebrate the Coronation of King Edward VII. The arrival of a photographer in the street was an event not to be missed. Compare that with a photograph of the street taken recently when I know for a certain fact that nobody even noticed the elderly bloke with his compact camera taking the photograph that is on page 43.

Left:
Fir Street. Walkley Reform Club. 1909. An example of the many political clubs that were a feature when politics was taken a lot more seriously than they are today with Liberal and Conservative Clubs predominating. This club started after the birth of the new Labour party and probably catered for its socialist members.
Photo taken in October 1978.

Right:
This chemists shop was No 284 South Road. The date is around 1912.

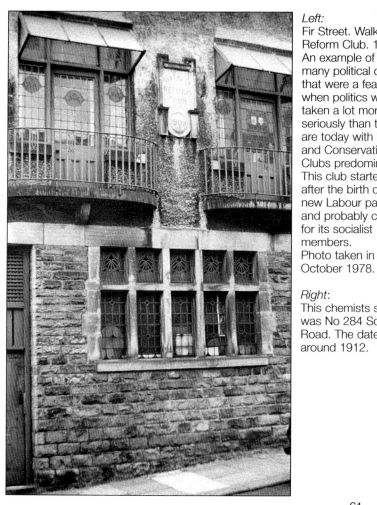

This is Greenhow Street as it was on the 19th June 1983. The Ebenezer Chapel Sunday School has the date over the doorway 1908. The chapel itself is a much older building probably dating from around 1880. The Ordnance Survey map for 1903 shows that the piece of land from which I took the photograph belonged to Walkley House and garden.

South Road around 1905. It was clearly the terminus as the lines end abruptly with no buffers - drivers needed to be alert in those days. The horse and cart owner and the Edwardian children are showing their contempt for these new-fangled contraptions.

The photographer of this postcard had his back to the city and is pointing his camera towards Walkley Road. By a co-incidence the same tram features in both views. Again the date is mid-Edwardian - say 1905.

Howard Road leading to South Road around 1909.

Howard Road around 1905 near Cromwell Street.
Notice the tramlines laid so that the trams could pass each
other on what was mainly a single track.

Howard Road looking towards Fulton Road. The huge wall acts as a retaining wall to the Catholic Hospital. The road leads down to South Road and in the distance can be seen St. Mary's Church spire. Taken the 17th July 1974.

This old photograph from 1901 was taken from Barber Road and shows Commonside at its junction with Sydney Road. The tall wall enclosed the grounds of Moor End House.

This is Commonside at Steel Bank. The single-deck tramcar suggests a date of 1905 or earlier. The Springfield pub can be seen beyond the shops.

The Old Cottage pub was on Bole Hill Road on the same site as where the Walkley Cottage pub now stands. I do not have an exact date for this photograph but it seems to date from the Edwardian period.
It was certainly well below street level.

Walkley Hall was situated on Heavygate Road just above Bole Hill Road. This photograph dates from around 1909.

Moor End House with the family and even the servants trying to get in on the act. For a picture of the house today see page 44 There has been some talk of a fire recently but I have not been able to confirm this. The date is around 1909.

This is Rivelin Street that runs down the hill towards Rivelin. It rivals Blake St. in being the steepest in Sheffield.

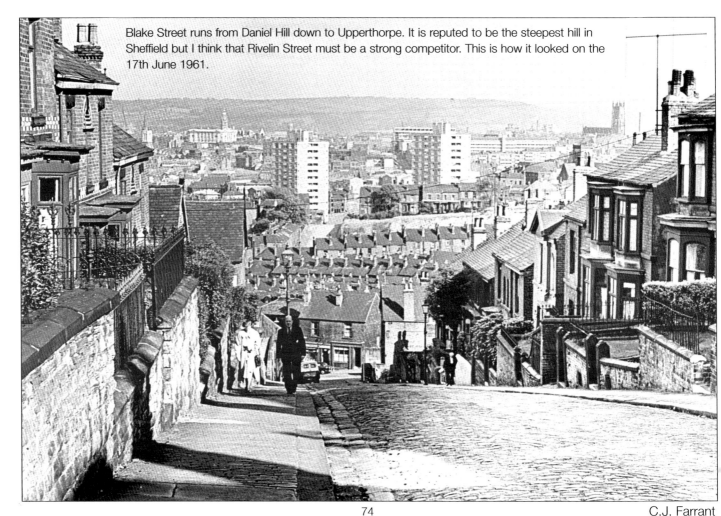

Blake Street runs from Daniel Hill down to Upperthorpe. It is reputed to be the steepest hill in Sheffield but I think that Rivelin Street must be a strong competitor. This is how it looked on the 17th June 1961.

C.J. Farrant

This shows Bole Hill Road along its length as it disappears into the beautiful Rivelin Valley.
I took the photograph on the 19th of June 1983.

Daniel Hill School here stands proudly aloft but possibly not for much longer. The school is no longer in use and the site was recently sold off. It looks as if another of the fine buildings commissioned by the Sheffield School Board will soon be a memory. The photo dates from 27th July 1974 when the school was still in use.

Fulton Road maintains a certain Rustic charm as this shot taken on 18th July 1974 shows. Formerly Prospect Road it was renamed in 1872 to avoid confusion with others of the same name.

Harworth Street is another lost street. Your Sheffield A to Z no longer shows it. It was already doomed when this photo was taken - the 23rd July 1974. The distant view of Burgoyne Road School gives the location away. It is under Ruskin Park that has been created opposite the school. Bloor Street - its neighbouring street - also suffered the same fate.

A view across Ponderosa recreation ground to Bramley St. and Mushroom Lane. It shows many of the back-to-back houses that have now almost completely disappeared. The date is 25th August 1965.

This is Langsett Rd. in 1970. On the left is the old police house in use by Goodley and Ball, the dentist. The pair of semis are now being replaced by a block of flats. On the right was the garage at the bottom of Primrose Hill.. Through the alley can be be seen St. Bartholomew's church.